CARPENTER MCQ

OBJECTIVE QUESTION ANSWERS

MANOJ DOLE

Copyright © Manoj Dole
All Rights Reserved.

Digitization is the need of the time. In the future, training in industrial training institutes will need to be conducted using online internet to make training more convenient and easy. E-books containing a set of MCQ questions will be made available to the trainees as they need to be more accustomed to the multiple choice questions MCQ to prepare for the online exams taking place in their industrial training institutes.

With all these factors in mind, Mr. Manoj Madhukar Dole Instructor, Industrial Training Institute, Satara, has written books according to the new annual system and NSQF-5 syllabus. And they've created theoretical mobile apps and blogs to make training easier, and made all these educational materials available for download on the world famous websites Google Play Store, Amazon and Apple Book Store.

The books were published by Hon'ble Joint Director Shri Rajendra Ghume Saheb Regional Office of Vocational Education and Training, Pune on 9/1/2019, at this time Shri Prakash Saigavkar Saheb Principal Government Industrial Training Institute Aundh Pune, Shri Tukaram Misal Saheb Principal Govt. Q. Sanstha Satara, Shri Sachin Dhumal Saheb District Vocational Education and Training Officer Satara, Shri Yatin Pargaonkar Saheb Principal Govt. Q. Sanstha Kolhapur, Shri Vikas Teke Saheb Inspector Vocational Education and Training Regional Office Pune, Palekar Foods Products Pvt. Ltd. Entrepreneurial Chairman of Satara Mr. Nilkanthrao Palekar Saheb, Chairman of Hira Foods Mr. Ibrahim Baba Tamboli Saheb, Mrs. Shalmali Pawar Headmaster Government Technical School Center Satara and other dignitaries were present on the occasion.

Contents

Prologue

Carpenter MCQ is a simple e-Book for ITI & Engineering Course Carpenter, Revised NSQ Syllabus in 2022, It contains objective questions with underlined & bold correct answers MCQ covering all topics including all about the latest & Important about makes, assembles, alters and repairs wooden structures and articles according to sample or drawing using hand or power tools or both. Studies drawing on sample to understand type of structure or article to be made and calculates quantity of timber required. Selects timber to suit requirements. Marks them to size using square, scriber etc. Saws, chisels and planes wooden pieces to required sizes and makes necessary joints such as half lap, Tenonmortice, dovetail etc. using saws, planes, mortising, chisels, drills and other carpentry hand or power tools as required. Checks parts frequently with square, foot rule, measuring tape etc. to ensure correctness. Assembles parts and secures them in position by screwing, nailing or doweling. Checks assembled structure with drawing or sample; rectifies defects, if any, and finishes it to required specifications. Alters, repairs or replaces components in case of old structures or articles in similar manner. May glue parts together. May smoothen and finish surface with sandpaper and polish. May fix metal fittings to structure and polish. May fix metal fittings to structure or article made. May calculate cost of furniture. May sharpen his own tools. Carpenter, Construction; Carpenter Building makes, assembles, alters and repairs doors, windows, frames and other wooden fixtures of building using hand or power tools or both. Studies drawings or samples and calculates quantity of timber required. Saws oversize pieces by power or hand tools or collects lumbers for making various components. Plans two sides of above pieces, marks off dimensions using tri-square, scriber, pencil etc., and reduces them to required sizes by adzing, sawing and planning. Marks off different members cuts them as required and shapes and makes Tenon and mortise, half lap and other joints by sawing, chiselling, drilling and filling. Checks pieces frequently while sizing and shaping to ensure correctness. Assembles framework step by step by gluing, cramping, dowelling, nailing and screwing as required. Examines finished article for accuracy. Fits metal rods, hinges etc., to wood work where necessary and rectifies defects in fittings if any. Sharpens his own tools. May erect scaffoldings if necessary. and lots more.

We add new question answers with each new version. Please email us in case of any errors/omissions. This is arguably the largest and best e-Book for All engineering multiple choice questions and answers.

As a student you can use it for your exam prep. This e-Book is also useful for professors to refresh material.

Foreword

Vocational education and training is imparted through the Department of Vocational Education and Training through the Department of Business Education and Business Practical to supply multi-skilled artisans in line with the rapidly growing demand in the industrial sector in the 21st century. All the occupations within the institutions are important, as the trainees from these occupations develop multi-skills as per the demands of the industry.

with the noble intention of making available MCQ e-books suitable for all businesses, considering that all the examinations in all the industries in the industrial sector are conducted online and include MCQ method questions. Mr. Manoj Madhukar Dole has written a very good e-book on MCQ method as per the new annual syllabus. This e-book will definitely be a guide for all the trainees, trainee candidates, training instructors and others concerned.

The author of the book is Mr. Manoj Madhukar Dole, Instructor Gov. ITI Satara has 17 years of training experience. Written as a new annual pattern, this e-book incorporates modern digital QR Code technology to understand the layout, simple language, and simple syntax, diagrams and videos for each subject. So I am sure that this e-book will definitely be useful for in-depth study and exam practice. The work they have done is certainly commendable.

Mr. Tukaram Misal
Principal Government Industrial Training Institute Satara.

Preface

DGET New Delhi and CSTARI Kolkata have been implementing an annual pattern for all businesses in ITI since the August 2018 session. The examination system will also be changed and it will be online from this year and since all the questions are of Objective Type (MCQ), the trainees are in dire need of in-depth study. It is with this in mind that we are delighted to present the books based on the old NIMI pattern and a complete overview of the new annual pattern, and we hope that these books will be a guide for all business directors and trainees. Is.

For writing these books, Johar Awate Saheb, Principal of ITI Akluj. Former Principal of ITI Satara Saigavkar Saheb, Assistant Director Shri Chandrakant Dhekne Saheb Regional Office of Vocational Education and Training, Pune, District Vocational Education and Training Officer Sachin Dhumal Saheb and Headmaster Government Technical School Kendra Shalmali Pawar Madam and son Adhiraj Dole, mother Kusum Dole, I am very grateful to my father Madhukar Dole and wife Ashwini Dole for their special guidance and cooperation from time to time.

Also, in a very short period of time, the book was reviewed by Shri Rajendra Ghume Saheb, Joint Director, Vocational Education and Training Regional Office, Pune, for his invaluable time in publishing the book. I am sincerely grateful for their feedback.

I am grateful to the Instructor of ITI Satara for there continuous support from the very beginning of writing the book.

From this book, I consider myself blessed to have shared my thoughts on e-learning with you. I will not claim that this book is perfect, because considering the perfection, this book is an attempt and is in its infancy. They will be valuable for improvement if they are tested and suggested.

Manoj Dole
Dated 9/1/2019

Acknowledgements

The industrial training and theoretical examination system of our industrial training institutes and these changes have been accepted by the craft instructors and the trainees. Theoretical examinations conducted in your industrial training institutes are also conducted online. Since these examinations are of multiple choice MCQ method, the trainees will need to get more practice of such questions.

With all these considerations in mind, Mr. Manoj Madhukar, Director, Dole Crafts, Katari Industrial Training Institute, Satara, has done a thorough study and with his diligent work and added his keen intellect, according to the new annual system and NSQF-5 syllabus, e-book of Katari and other machine trades. -Book) and they have created mobile apps and blogs on theoretical topics to make training easier and have made all these educational materials available for download on the world famous websites Google Play Store, Amazon and Apple Book Store. Training has been made easier by creating a print version and using advanced techniques like QR Code.

All these educational materials will definitely be a guide for all the trainees for in-depth study and for the craft instructors and other concerned who are imparting vocational training.

Carpenter MCQ Drawing

Download App
Online Test Exam
ITI Books
AutoCAD CAM
JOB & Apprentice
Online Theory
Computer Course
Trading Course
CNC Course
MSCIT Course
Shopping Business
Internet Business
Web Designing
Online Services
Top Sportsmans
Indian Army
Freedom Fighters
Top Scientists
Social Reformers
Motivational Speaker
Top Richest People
Join WhatsApp Group
Join Facebook Group
Like Facebook Page
PAN / Adhar / Licence Passport

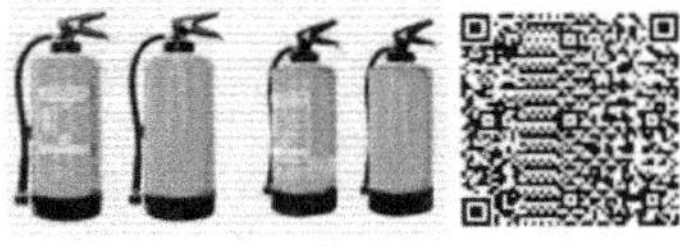

Fire extinguisher

Calliper

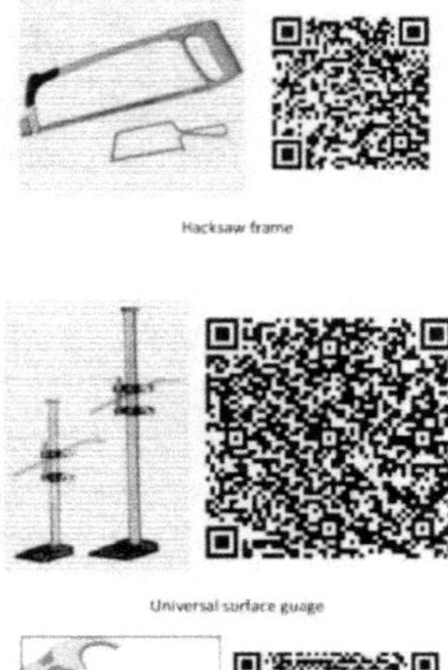

Hacksaw frame

Universal surface guage

Hammer

• 5 •

Centre punch

Bench vice

Files

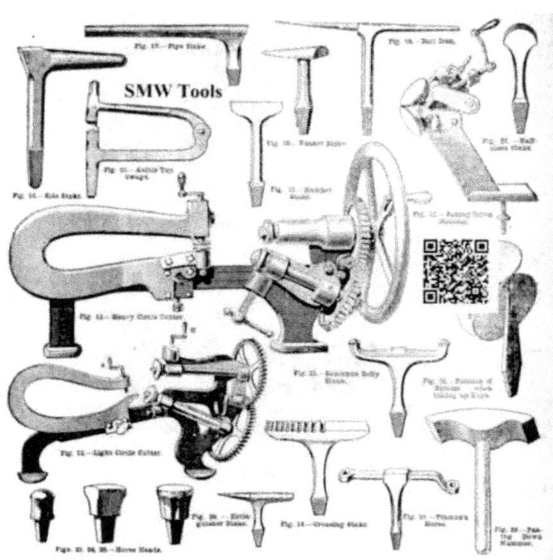
SMW Tools

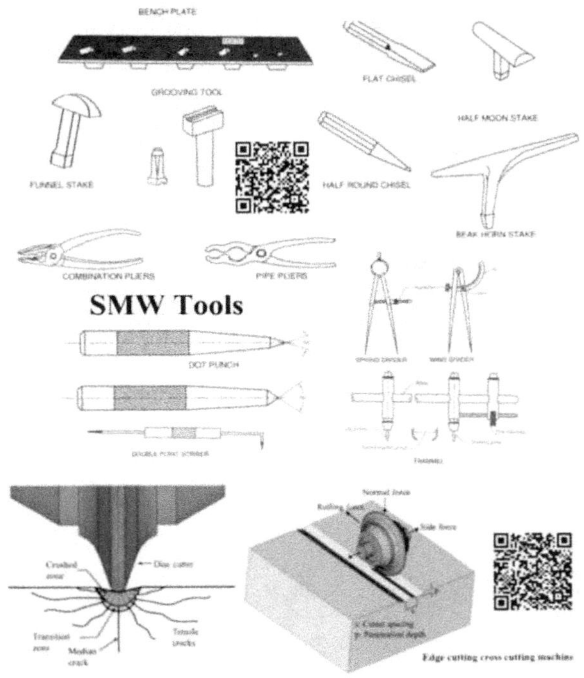

BENCH PLATE
FLAT CHISEL
GROOVING TOOL
HALF MOON STAKE
FUNNEL STAKE
HALF ROUND CHISEL
BEAK HORN STAKE
COMBINATION PLIERS
PIPE PLIERS
SMW Tools
DOT PUNCH
DOUBLE POINT SCRIBER
Edge cutting cross cutting machine

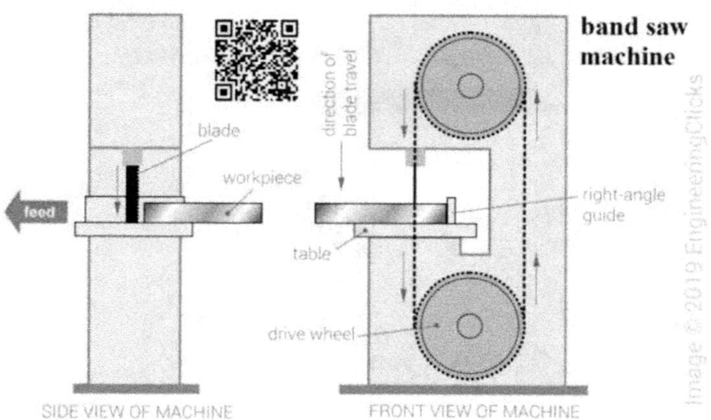
band saw
machine
blade
workpiece
feed
direction of
blade travel
right-angle
guide
table
drive wheel
SIDE VIEW OF MACHINE
FRONT VIEW OF MACHINE
Image © 2019 EngineeringClicks

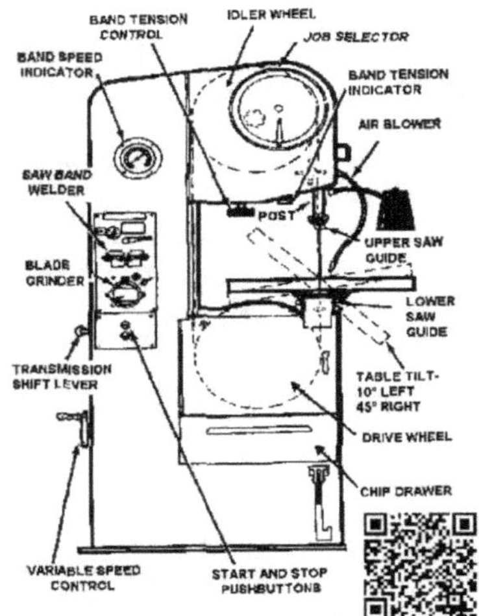

Figure 6-2. Vertical band sawing mach

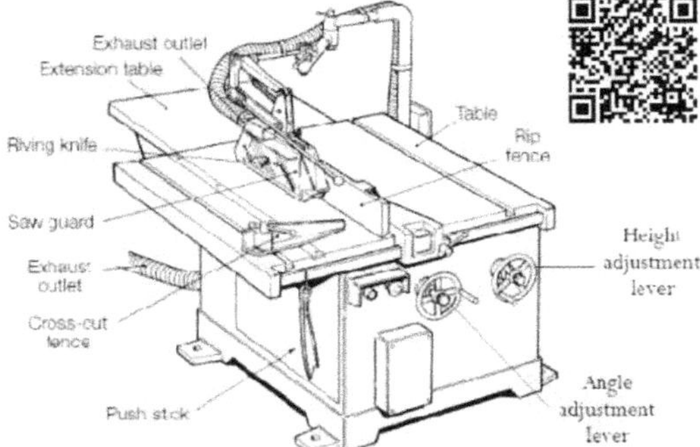

circular saw machine.

Workshop Tools
drill
pipe wrench
monkey wrench
clamp
chisel
anvil
wrench / spanner
shears
ruler
adhesive tape
measuring tape
drill bit
sandpaper
paint brush
toolbox
hacksaw
nail
saw
spirit level
awl
extension cord
hammer
screw
circular saw
screwdriver
chain saw
mallet
glue
file
pliers

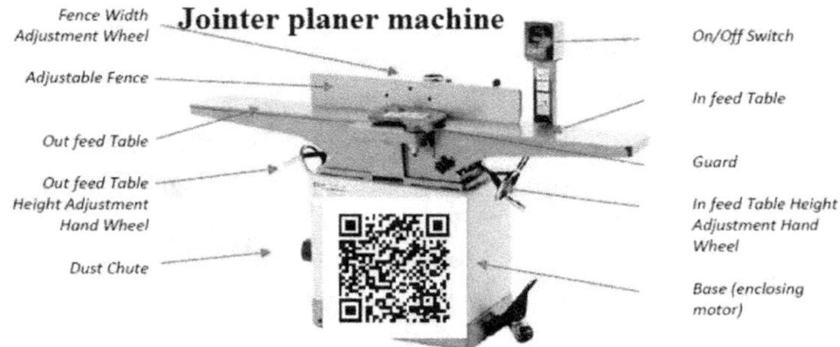
Fence Width Adjustment Wheel
Adjustable Fence
Out feed Table
Out feed Table Height Adjustment Hand Wheel
Dust Chute
Jointer planer machine
On/Off Switch
In feed Table
Guard
In feed Table Height Adjustment Hand Wheel
Base (enclosing motor)

Mortise machine

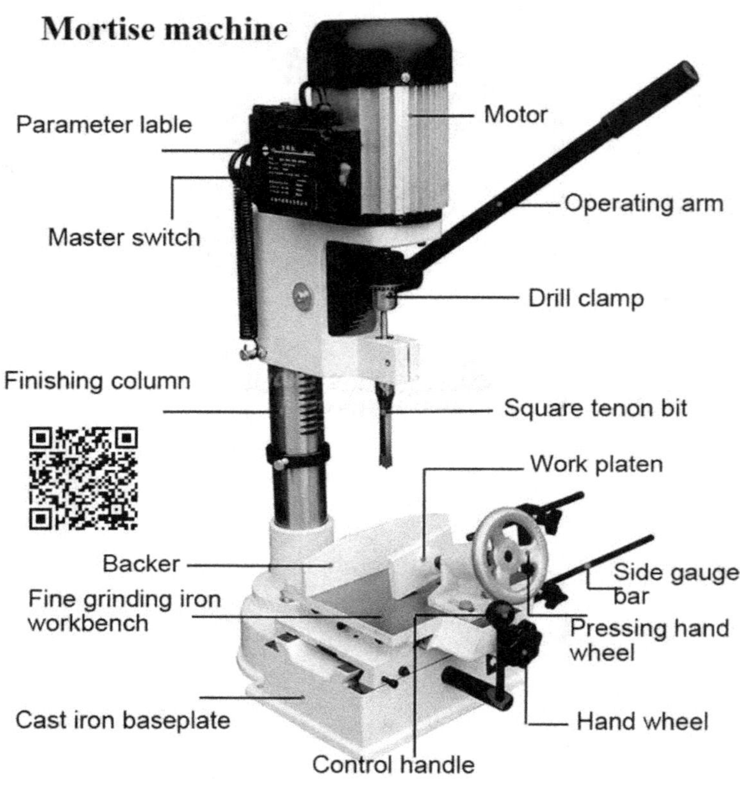

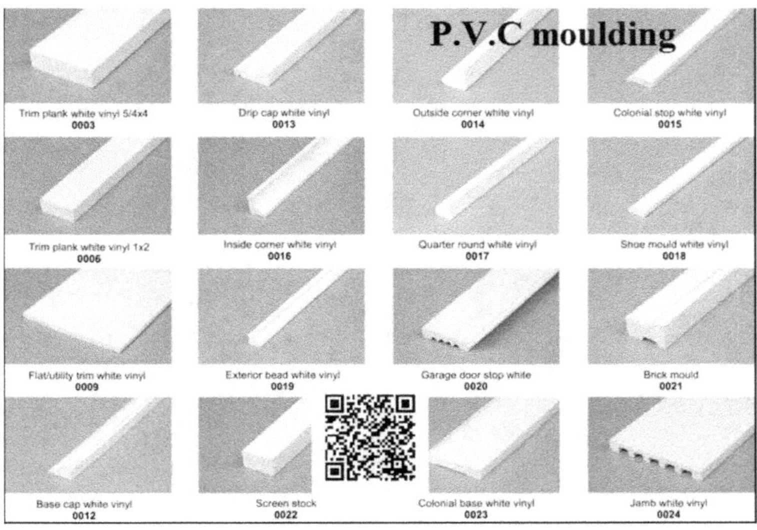

P.V.C moulding
Trim plank white vinyl 5/4x4
0003
Drip cap white vinyl
0013
Outside corner white vinyl
0014
Colonial stop white vinyl
0015
Trim plank white vinyl 1x2
0006
Inside corner white vinyl
0016
Quarter round white vinyl
0017
Shoe mould white vinyl
0018
Flat/utility trim white vinyl
0009
Exterior bead white vinyl
0019
Garage door stop white
0020
Brick mould
0021
Base cap white vinyl
0012
Screen stock
0022
Colonial base white vinyl
0023
Jamb white vinyl
0024

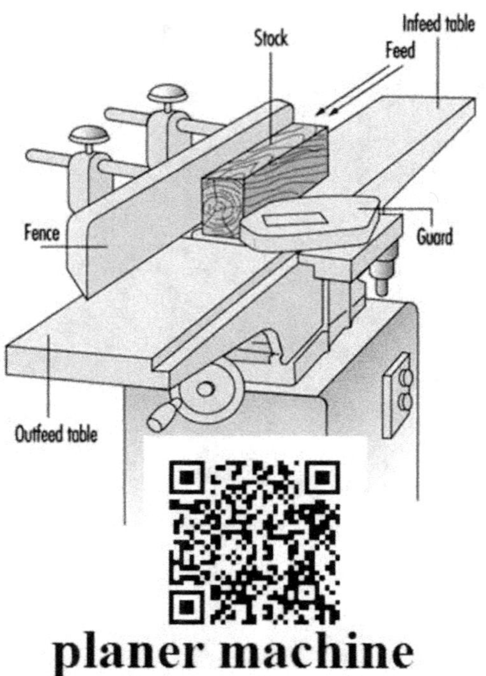

planer machine

• 15 •

portable circular saw machine

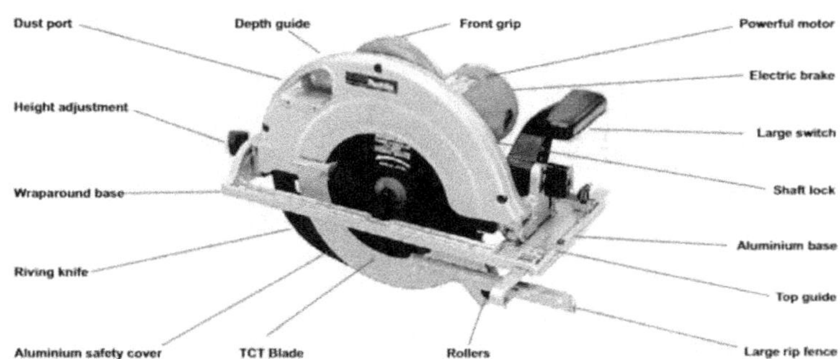

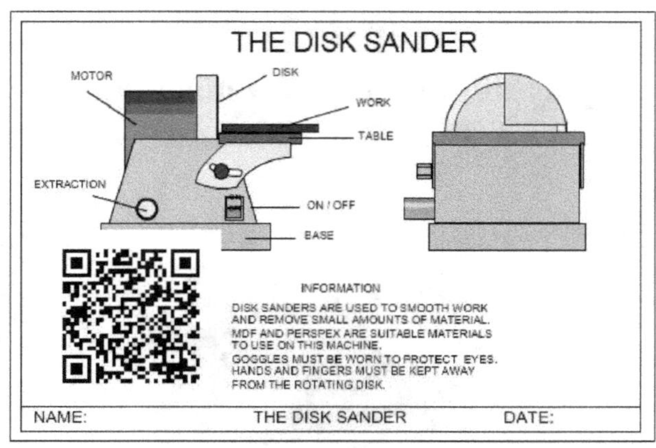

portable power planer machine

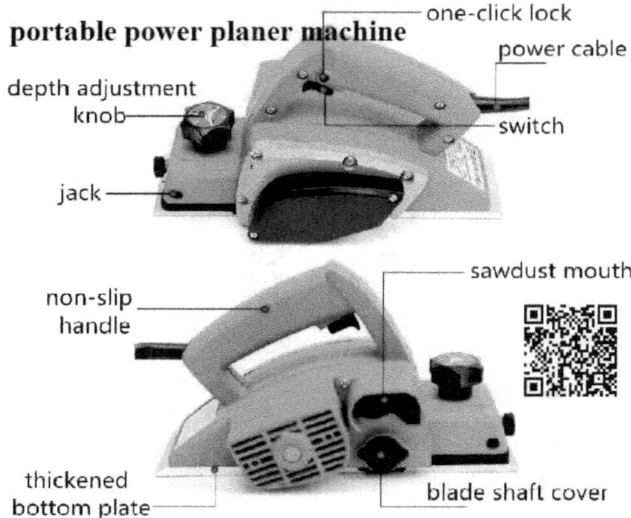

Palm grip
Portable sander machine
Power cable
Power switch
D-handle
Body (housing motor)
BLACK&DECKER
Lip seal
Sanding pad
Dust bag

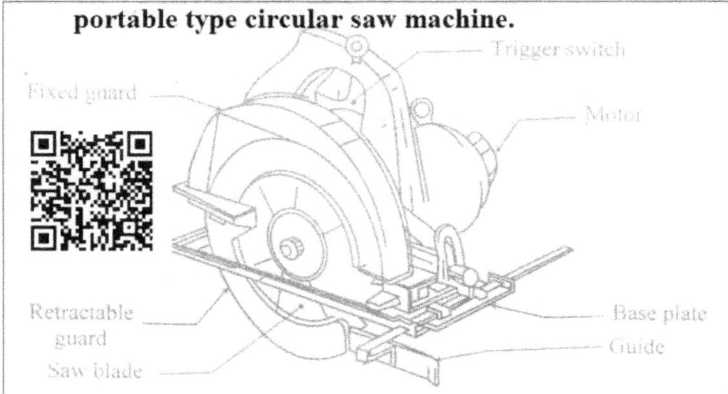
portable type circular saw machine.
Trigger switch
Fixed guard
Motor
Retractable guard
Base plate
Guide
Saw blade

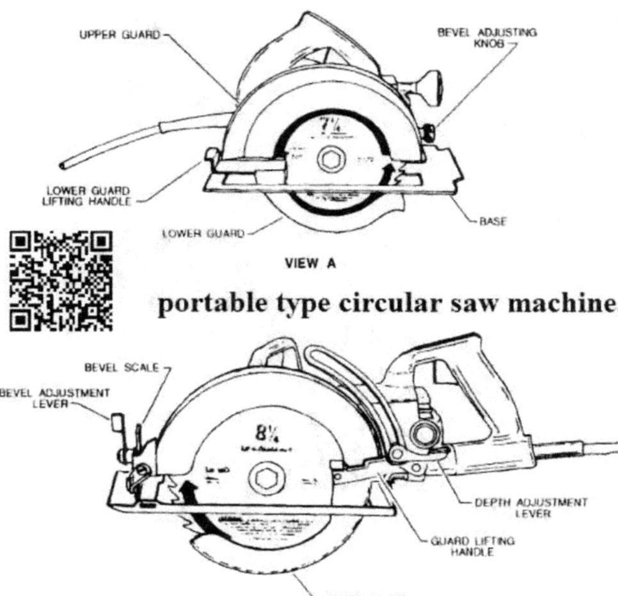

portable type circular saw machine.

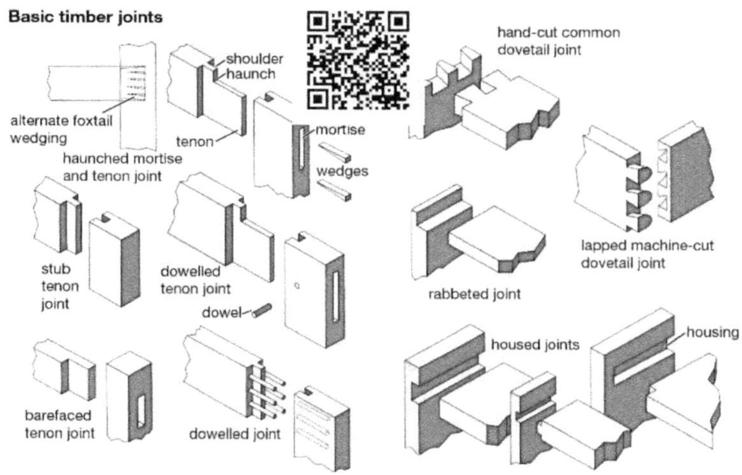

Basic timber joints
shoulder
haunch
alternate foxtail wedging
tenon
mortise
wedges
haunched mortise and tenon joint
stub tenon joint
dowelled tenon joint
dowel
barefaced tenon joint
dowelled joint
hand-cut common dovetail joint
lapped machine-cut dovetail joint
rabbeted joint
housed joints
housing

Crosscut saw
Backsaw
Jack plane
Block plane
Surform plane
Miter box
Utility knife
Screwdrivers
Wood chisels
Rasps
Coping saw
Sanding block
Finishing hammer
Long-nose pliers
Nail set
Groove-joint pliers
Spade bits
Brad-point bits
Hand drill
Dead blow hammer
Forstner bits
Twist bits
Drill-stop collars
Dowel centers

Hand Tools

Window shutter
REGULAR PUSH ROD
HIDDEN PUSH ROD SYSTEM
TOP RAIL
FRAME
STILE
MID RAIL
PUSH ROD
SLATS
MOUSEHOLE
BOTTOM RAIL
TOP RAIL
FRAME
STILE
MID RAIL
HIDDEN PUSH ROD
SLATS
BOTTOM RAIL

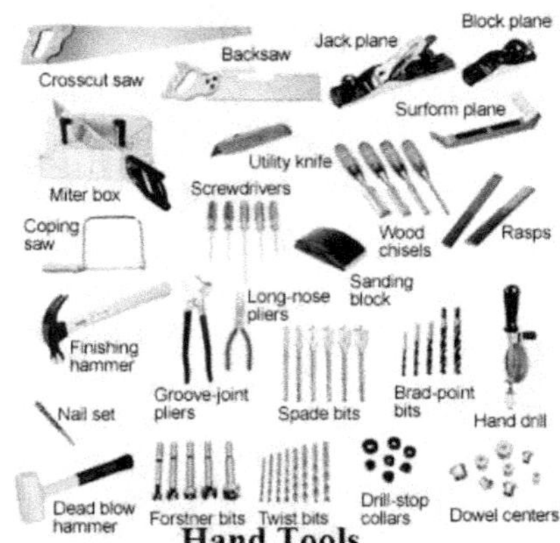

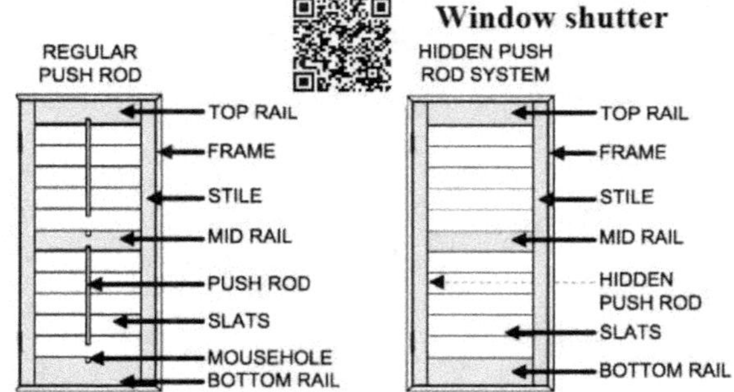

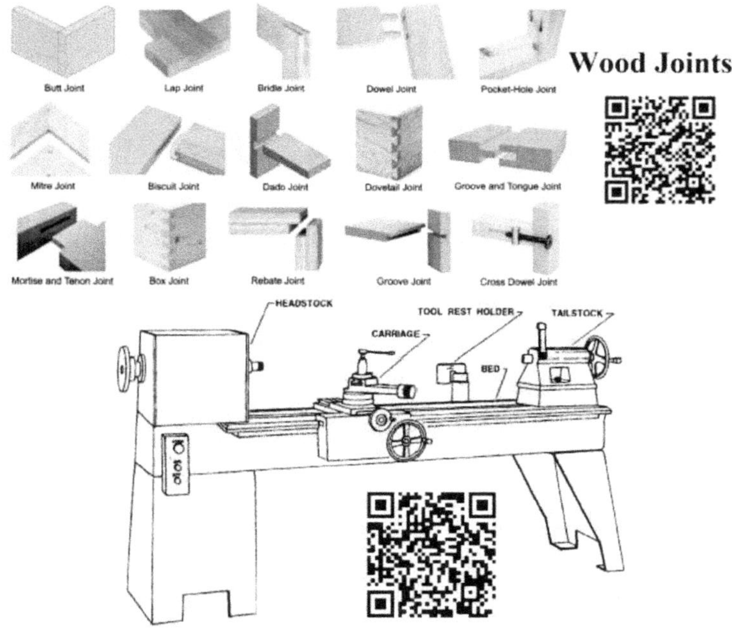

Wood Joints

Wood Turning Lathe

CHAPTER TWO

1] Which one is a workshop safety?

A] <u>Keep shop floor clean and free from grease, oil or other slippery materials</u>

B] Stop the machine before changing the speed

C] Don't use cracked or chipped tools

D] Don't try to stop a running machine with hand

2] In Personal Protect Equipment (PPE] HELMET is used to

A] <u>protect head</u>

B] Protect eyes

C] Protect hands

D] Protect ears

3] Which of the following belongs to general safety?

A Have a worker in good attitude

B] The work clean and clear

C] Concentrate on your work

D] <u>Keep the floor and gangways clean and clear</u>

4] While grinding, which is used to protect the eyes?

A] Dark green glass

B] Mask

C] Sun glasses

D] <u>Safety goggles</u>

5] Which of the following is done for machine safety?

A] <u>Check the oil level before starting the machine</u>

B] Do things in a methodical way

C] Keep the floor and gangways clean and clear

D] Don't use dies and scarves

6] In Personal Protect Equipment (PPE], 'sleeves' is used to protect ----------

A] Face

B] Eyes

C] Ears

D] Hands

7] ABC stands for --------------

A] Automatic Breathing Control

B] Automatic Blood Control

C] Airway Breathing Circulation

D] Automatic Blood Circulation

8] Fire & FIRE EXTINGUISHERS

Fire extinguisher

9] To put off"Class B" fire, the types of fire extinguisher used is ....

A] dry power

B] Carbon dioxide

C] Jet of water

D] Foam type

10] Which type of fire extinguisher is used to put off general fire?

A] Water type Extinguisher

B] Foam type Extinguisher

C] Dry chemical powder Extinguisher

D] Carbon dioxide (C02] Extinguisher

11] In case of bleeding, take treatment Of

D] cold 3" and rest

A] spray cold water

B] Bandage immediately -----.

B] Enquire about the accident thought treatment

12] in case of an accident, the victim should im
A] Asked to take rest
C] Attended immediately
D] leave him
13] First aid is given to an injured or ill person primarily....
A] Save life
B] Prevent further deterioration of the muff's
C] Give best possible comfort
D] All of these
14] Colour code for Bins for waste paper segregation is -----
A] blue Colour
B] Yellow Colour
C] Red Colour
D] Green Colour
15] In Japanese Seiko stands for --------------
A] Shine
B] Sort
C] Standardize
D] Sustain
16] Benefit of SS system is ------
A] Increase in productivity
B] Increase in quality
C] Reduction in wastage of time
D] All of these
17] Safety is -----------
A] nobody's business
B] every bodise business
C] Some bodies business
D] The organization business
18] For basic categories of safety signs are available The meaning of"prohibition" sign ----

A] shows it must not be done

B] Shows what must be done

C] Warns the hazard or danger

D] Gives information of safety provision

18] One micrometer (U] is equal to...

A] 0.1mm

B] 0.01mm

C] 0.001mm

D] 0.0001mm

19] The caliper meant for measuring the width of a slot is...

A] Odd leg caliper

B] Outside caliper

C] Jenny caliper

D] Inside calliper

Calliper

20] The size of the dividers are specified by the -----------

A] Total length of legs

B] Distance between the points when fully opened

C] Length of legs without points

D] distance between the pivot and the point

21] The instrument used to mark parallel lines, parallel to the datum edge is -

A] jenny caliper

B] Divider

C] Outside calliper

D] Inside calliper

22] Which one of the following is an indirect measuring tool?

A] Outside caliper

B] Vernier calliper

C] Steel rule

D] Outside micrometer

23] For cutting thin tubing, the most suitable pitch of the hacksaw blade is...

A] 1.8mm

B] 1.4mm

C] 1mm

D] <u>0.8mm</u>

24] For cutting solid brass, the most suitable pitch of the hacksaw blade is...

A] <u>1.8mm</u>

B] 1.4mm

C] 1mm

D] 0.8mm

Hacksaw frame

25] A new hacksaw blade after a few strokes becomes loose because of the...

A] <u>Stretching of the blade</u>

B] Wing-nut threads being worn out

C] Wrong pitch of the blade

D] Improper selection of the set of saws.

26] While cutting small diameter pipes, it is advisable to watch regularly and ensure that...

A] The cut is along the curved line

B] <u>More saw teeth are in contract</u>

C] The work is not overheated

D] Proper balancing of hacksaw is maintained

27] The vice clamps are used to...

A] Protect hard jaws

B] Clamp the work pieces rigidly

C] <u>Protect the finished surfaces</u>
D] Prevent the movable jaw being filed
28] The reference surface during marking is provided by the...
A] Surface gauge
B] Workpiece
C] Drawing of the work
D] <u>Marking table surface</u>
29] The size of an engineer's vice is specified by the...
A] Length of the movable jaw
B] <u>Width of the jaws</u>
C] Height of the vice
D] Maximum opening of the jaws
30] The part of the universal surface gauge which helps to draw a parallel line along a datum edge is the..
A] Rocker arm
B] Snug
C] Fine adjustment screw
D] <u>Guide pins</u>

Universal surface guage

31] Scribers are made of...
A] Mild steel
B] <u>High carbon steel</u>
C] Brass
D] Cast iron
32] Portion of the hammer used for fixing the handle is...
A] Face

B] Peen

C] Cheek

D] <u>Eye hole</u>

33] Weight of the hammer for the marking purpose is...

A] <u>250g</u>

B] 500g

C] 1 kg

D] 2 kgs

Hammer

34] The size of the dividers are specified by the...

A] Total length of the legs

B] Distance between the points when fully opened

C] Length of legs without the points

D] <u>Distance between the pivot and the point</u>

35] The included angle of the groove of 'V' block is always....

A] 45°

B] 60°

C] 90°

D] <u>120°</u>

36] 'V' blocks are available in grades of...

A] <u>A & B</u>

B] A,B & C

C] 1,2 & 3

D] 1 & 2

37] 'V' blocks of grade 'B' are made of

A] <u>Cast iron</u>

B] Mild steel

C] Steel

D] Cast steel

38] Name the punch used to locate the centre.

A] Prick punch 30°

B] Prick punch 60°

C] Centre punch

D] Dot punch

Centre punch

39] The point angle of centre punch is --------

A] 30°

B] 50°

c] 900

D] 1200

40] Punches are used for forming ---------of any shape

A] Holes

B] Mining

C] Knurling

D] Reaming

41] Generally the length of the handle of the vice is ----------

A] 1.5 times the normal size of the vice

B] 2.5 times the normal size of the vice

C] 3.5 times the normal size of the vice

D] 4.5 times the normal size of the vice

Bench vice

42] Bench vice spindle is made of ....

A] mild steel

B] Cast iron

C] Tool steel

D] Bronze

43] The convexity of files helps...

A] To file concave surfaces

B] To file convex surfaces

C] To prevent rounding of edges of work

D] The file to become straight when pressure is applied

Files

44] Which file used for filling wood, leather and other soft material? .

A] Single cut file

B] Double cut file

c] Rasp cut file

D] Curved cut file

45] File used is used for ------------

A] Cleaning the work piece

C] Renewing the file teeth
B] cleaning the file teeth
D] Cleaning the chips
46] File card is used to --------
A] Clean the work piece
C] Renew the file teeth
B] Clean the file teeth
47] The point angle of scriber is -----------
A] 30°
B] 60°
C] 5° to 10°
D] 12° to 15°
48] The cutting angle for chipping cast iron is...
A] 37.5°
B] 55°
C] 60°
D] 90°

49] The chisel will dig into the material when...
A] The rake angle is more
B] The clearance angle is too low
C] The angle of inclination is more
D] The angle of inclination is too low
50] A slight convexity is given to the cutting edge to...
A] Cut curved surfaces
B] Cut sharp corners
C] Prevent digging of the ends
D] Allow the lubricant to enter
51] Surface plates are made of...
A] High grade cast steel
B] Fine-grained cast iron
C] Alloy steels

D] Wrought iron

52] Surface plates are specified by their length and breadth & are in
A] decimetre
B] Cubic meter
C] Cylindrical
53] Ribs are given on the unmachined portion of the angle plate for...
A] Easy handling
B] Convenience in manufacturing
C] Clamping while setting on machines
D] Rigidity and to prevent distortion
54] The slots on the angle plate are given for...
A] Reducing weight
B] Aligning the work
C] Lifting using hooks
D] Accommodating bolts.
55] The size of the angle plates is stated by...
A] Weight
B] Length
C] Length x width
D] Size number
Q 1) The first formed round dark portion of the tree is called ....
A) Ring
B) Pith
C) Bark
D) Cortex
Q 2) Which of the following can resist attack by white ants?
A) Deodar
B) Teak
C) Chir
D) Kail

Q 3) Which saw would be best choice for cutting an opening in wallboard for a switch box?

A) Key hole saw

B) Coping saw

C) Hacksaw

D) Back saw

Q 4) Name the part of the band saw machine which is provided between the wheels to support the work piece.

A) Table

B) Arm

C) Guide post

D) Column

Q 5) When a tree grows, many of its branches fall and the stump of these branches in the trunk is covered. In the

sawn pieces of timber the stump of fallen branches appear as ....

A) Spot

B) Knot

C) Ridge

D) Wedge

Q 6) In the figure given below, which one is dovetail joint?

A) Joint A

B) Joint B

C) Joint C

D) Joint D

Q 7) Identify what is shown in figure given below.

A) Pins

B) Ribs

C) Dowels

D) Keys

Q 8) Which of these joints is so weak that it has to be reinforced with steel plates or brackets when building roof

trusses?

A) Dovetail joint

B) Bridle joint

C) Butt joint

D) Mortise and tenon joint

Q 9) The distance from a given point on one thread to the corresponding point on the next thread is called ....

A) Helix
B) Lead
C) Pitch
D) Flat
Q 10) Which type of lock is NOT permanently attached to the door?
A) Pad lock
B) Knob lock
C) Deadbolt
D) Camlock
Q 11) A clicking noise on a band saw indicates ....
A) A broken wheel guard
B) A crack in the blade
C) Electrical power tripping
D) Nothing wrong
Q 12) What is the type of hinge shown in figure given below?
A) Butt hinge
B) Lift off hinge
C) Flush hinge
D) Security butt hinge
Q 13) The size of a tablesaw is determined by the ....
A) Height of the table
B) Shaft diameter
C) Blade diameter
D) Blade width
Q 14) The box shown in figure given below is called ....
A) Carpenter s box
B) Shaping box
C) Slitting box
D) Mitre box
Q 15) The tool used to test squareness of wood is ....
A) Ruler
B) Framing square
C) Try square
D) Combination square
Q 16) What is used to extract nails?
A) Ball pein hammer
B) Claw hammer
C) Mallet

D) Sledge hammer

Q 17) Figure below shows a piece of wood held in a vice. When using a plane, which direction should it move?

A) From left to right

B) From right to left

C) In any direction

D) Direction of movement is not important

Q 18) Which tool is used to make a fine cut in wooden workpiece?

A) Hand saw

B) Wooden saw

C) Tenon saw

D) Rip saw

Q 19) Which statement is NOT true with respect to the tool shown in figure below?

A) It is called brace

B) It is used with auger bits

C) It is used for drilling small diameter holes

D) It allows a lot of force to be applied to the drill bit

Q 20) Freshly cut lumber that has not been dried is called ....

A) Raw lumber

B) Fresh lumber

C) Green lumber

D) Base lumber

Q 21) The marks put on boards or pieces to keep them in order during gluing, joining and assembly, are called

....

A) Assembly marks

B) Witness marks

C) Visible marks

D) Limiting marks

Q 22) The post (figure given below) at the top or bottom of a stairway that supports the handrail, is called ....

A) Newel

B) Muntin

C) Ogee

D) Mould

Q 23) The angle at which the leading edge of the teeth are cut on a saw blade, is called

A) Face

B) Rake

C) Cutting angle

D) Clearance angle

Q 24) The kind of door used in fire exits is ....

A) Double action door

B) Panel door with panic bar

C) Panel door

D) Revolving door

Q 25) The disadvantage of sliding door is .... of cabinet opening is available.

A) One-half

B) One-third

C) One-fourth

D) One-fifth

Q 26) The upper most member of a door frame is called ....

A) Door head

B) Door roller

C) Door closer

D) Door jamb

Q 27) The member which is placed horizontally to support common rafter of a sloping roof, is ....

A) Purlin

B) Cleat

C) Batten

D) Strut

Q 28) Which of these is NOT a type of truss?

A) King post truss

B) Queen post truss

C) Prince post truss

D) Pratt truss

Q 29) The outer protective layer of a tree is called ....

A) Bark

B) Bast

C) Cambium

D) Sap wood

Q 30) The ratio of rise to span of a truss is called ....

A) Scale

B) Lead

C) Peak

D) Pitch

Q 31) A tool similar to an axe with the blade perpendicular to the handle, used to carve wood, is called ....

A) Awl

B) Adze

C) Scraper

D) Gouge

Q 32) When you use a chisel, it is important that you ....

A) Keep both hands behind all the times

B) Hit harder if chisel is blunt

C) Chisel across the grains if possible

D) Use the biggest possible chisel at all the times

Q 33) Which tool can produce mouldings, trim edges, form recesses and cut grooves?

A) Jack plane

B) Belt sander

C) Reciprocating saw

D) Router

Q 34) A jointer is a tool designed to ....

A) Cut mitres

B) Apply glue

C) Plane surfaces

D) Rip narrow stock

Q 35) It is a knife which has blade between two handles. The handles are at right angles to the blade. It is used to

smooth a surface by pulling the blade over the stock. Name the tool.

A) Pullknife

B) Drawknife

C) Right angle knife

D) Bridge knife

Q 36) A hxagonal wrench is also known as ....

A) Allen wrench

B) Stillson wrench

C) Socket wrench

D) Ratchet wrench

Q 37) Figure given below shows two types of ....

A) Casters

B) Cambers

C) Rollers

D) Drag wheels

Q 38) The preferable way to cut the ends of a number of boards at the same angle is to use ....

A) Mitre box

B) Protractor

C) Combination square

D) Combination bevel

Q 39) You have a short section of lumber which you want to round off. Name the suitable file for this work.

A) Single cut

B) Double cut

C) Curved cut

D) Rasp cut

Q 40) Black sandpaper used to smooth metal and take off rust is ....

A) Emery

B) Aluminium oxide

C) Silicon carbide

D) Pumice

Q 41) Which of these is NOT an abrasive mineral used in woodworking?

A) Garnet

B) Ceramic

C) Silicon carbide

D) Calcium carbide

Q 42) Before turning wood on a lathe, make sure it is ....

A) Hardwwood

B) Free of saw dust

C) Free of defects

D) Softwood

Q 43) What adjustment on wood turning lathe you should make before sanding or polishing?

A) Move the tool rest closer to the stock

B) Remove the tool rest

C) Add lighting to the work area

D) Add a second tool rest

Q 44) What can help prevent slips and falls on shop floor?

A) Using short ladders

B) Wearing leather soled shoes

C) Keeping the floor free of clutter and wiping up spills

D) Keeping an even layer of sawdust on the floor

Q 45) When the safety rules refer to horseplay ,

A) Fooling around

B) Throwing things around

C) Animals on shop floor

D) Playing game of horses

Q 46) When using a plane, make adjustments carefully because the blade is ....

A) Soft

B) Beakable

C) Sharp

D) Expensive

Q 47) A thin layer of expensive wood bonded to a thicker piece of cheaper plywood to give the appearance of the expensive wood but at reduced price is called .....

A) Copse

B) Veneer

C) Thicket

D) Lumber

Q 48) A liquid preparation that dries to a hard lustrous coating is ....

A) Wax

B) Primer

C) Varnish

D) Sticker

Q 49) What is f in the wood turning lathe shown in figure given below?

A) Headstock

B) Lock knob

C) Tool post

D) Tailstock

Q 50) What type of surface is produced when facing operation is done on a lathe?

A) Flat

B) Taper

C) Cylindrical

D) Conical

Q 51) What might you use to hold together two pieces of wood if you are planning to glue them?

A) Hex tool

B) Biscuit joiner

C) C - clamp

D) Lever

Q 52) In CNC machines, the mode .... Is helpful when you are trying out a new program.

A) MDI

B) Single block

C) Edit

D) Initializing

Q 53) Plumb bob is used to verify the ....

A) Horizontal level

B) Vertical level

C) Parallel level

D) Surface level

Q 54) Which of the the following fire extinguisher is suitable for electrical fire?

A) Dry chemicals

B) Water

C) Foam

D) Soda acid

Q 55) Water is used to extinguish__________.

A) Class-A fires

B) Class-B fires

C) Class-C fires

D) All of these

Q 56) Which one of the following is not a type of straight cutting saw?

A) Bow saw

B) Rip saw

C) Tenon saw

D) Dovetail saw

Q 57) Which tool is used by carpenter sawing along the grains?

A) Plane

B) Chisel

C) Rip saw

D) Hammer

Q 58) Compared to other types of saws, tenon saws have________________.

A) More teeth per inch

B) Less teeth per inch

C) Same teeth per inch

D) None of these

Q 59) What is the use of circular saw ?

A) Ripping

B) Mitre cutting

C) Bevel cutting

D) All of these

Q 60) The length of the trying plane is____________.

A) 600-700 mm

B) 700-800 mm

C) 450-500 mm

D) 800-900 mm

Q 61) Which part indicate the age of a tree?

A) Pith

B) Ring

C) Bark

D) Cortex

Q 62) What is the scientific name of wood?

A) Xylem

B) Xylastrus orbiculatus

C) Parenchyma

D) Cycadophyta

Q 63) Which of the following is an example of soft wood?

A) Deodar

B) Sal

C) Oak

D) Mahogany

Q 64) The cracking on the outside of a log due to shrinkage of exterior surface is called________________.

A) Wind crack

B) Ring shake

C) Upset

D) Wane

Q 65) Which of the following is not a type of Chisel ?

A) Hot chisels

B) Bench chisels

C) Butt chiselz

D) Cabinet chisels

Q 66) The quality of timber does not depend upon_____________.

A) Size of tree

B) Maturity of tree

C) Weight of timber

D) Type of tree

Q 67) Identify the hand tool shown in the figure?

A) Gimlet

B) Screwdriver

C) Star-head Screwdriver

D) Flat nose plier

Q 68) Identify the hand tool shown in the figure?

A) Hand drill

B) Gimlet

C) Ratchet brace

D) Electric drill

Q 69) The_____________ joint is used in high quality furniture drawer construction.

A) Lapped dovetail

B) Rabbit

C) Dado

D) Lap

Q 70) which one of the following is a box joint?

A) Comb joint

B) Tee halving

C) Corner halving

D) Tenon and mortise

Q 71) _____________________ joints are employed to extend the length of a member by joining two pieces of timber.

A) Lengthening

B) Angle

C) Lapped

D) Widening

Q 72) Density is calculated by_______.

A) Mass ÷ Volume

B) Volume ÷ Mass

C) Volume X Mass

D) Weight X Thickness

Q 73) Which of the following is a part of screw driver?

A) Blade

B) Tip

C) Shank

D) All of these

Q 74) Identify the hand tool shown in the figure?

A) Pincer

B) Combination plier

C) Tong

D) Flat nose plier

Q 75) Which conversion method is shown in figure given below?

A) Tangential sawing

B) Parallel sawing

C) Radial sawing

D) Quarter sawing

Q 76) Fiber board are also known as ________________.

A) Pressed wood

B) Passed wood

C) Light wood

D) None of these

Q 77) A thin sheet of wood rotary cut, sliced or sawn from a log used as a superior facing to inferior wood to form

plywood is____________.

A) Veneer

B) Particle sheet

C) Cross bond layer

D) Vinyl sheet

Q 78) It is made by bonding together thin layers of wood in a way that the grains of each layer are at right angles

of the adjacent layer. It is____________.

A) Plywood

B) Building wood

C) Cork board

D) Hard board

Q 79) Which layer is called "core" in plywood?

A) Middle layer

B) Upper layer

C) Top layer

D) Side layer

Q 80) Which one of the statement is not an advantage of plywood?

A) It will shrink and warp easily

B) It is manufactured in very large size

C) It is lighter in weight

D) It can be easily worked and bent in shaped and designs

Q 81) Which part of the tree is mostly useful for carpentry work?

A) Heart wood

B) Sap wood

C) Bark

D) Root

Q 82) Which vice is used for sharpening the saw ?

A) saw vice

B) carpenter vice

C) Bar clamp

D) C- clamp

Q 83) Which of the following is not a preservative of timber?

A) Glue

B) Tar

C) Creosote

D) Chemical salt

Q 84) The angle of single cut file is________.

A) 60°

B) 51°

C) 70°

D) 90°

Q 85) A file used to make saw pointed is_________.

A) Triangular file

B) Half round file

C) Irregular file

D) Auger bit file

Q 86) "Knot" is a kind of defect in timber, which happens due to ___________.

A) Natural cause

B) Seasoning

C) Attack by fungi

D) Attack by insects

Q 87) Which is the most rapid and effective method of seasoning?

A) Electric seasoning

B) Kiln seasoning

C) Natural seasoning

D) Chemical seasoning

Q 88) Which of the following is a type of non-refractory timber?

A) Deoder

B) Teak

C) Sheesham

D) Sal

Q 89) __________________ joint is the simplest form of carpentry joint.

A) Dovetail

B) Rabbit

C) Finger

D) Lap

Q 90) What type of wood is best for furniture?

A) Cherry

B) White Oak

C) Pine

D) Teak

Q 91) Identify the chair shown in the figure.

A) Wood armed chair

B) Steel armed chair

C) Wood armless chair

D) Wood stool

Q 92) Which of the following is a type of circular saw blade?

A) Crosscut

B) Ripping

C) Combination

D) All of these

Q 93) Which one of the sawing operation is not related to circular saw machine?

A) Rip saw

B) Mould cutting

C) Miter cutting

D) Cross cutting

Q 94) Before planing, we must inspect the surface for_____________.

A) Turning
B) Warping
C) Correct dimensions
D) Trimming
Q 95) The maximum tiling angle of the band saw machine is________.
A) 45°
B) 60°
C) 90°
D) 120°
Q 96) Band saw sizes are determined by the_____________.
A) Wheel diameter
B) Blade thickness
C) Table size
D) None of these
Q 97) Hollow chisel mortising machine combines the cuting of a ____________ chisel with the action of the drill
bit in the centre.
A) Four-sided
B) Two-sided
C) Three-sided
D) None of these
Q 98) Mortiser machine is a _____________ machine, which is used to drill square and rectangular in
timber.
A) Wood working
B) Metal working
C) Clay working
D) None of these
Q 99) What is the name of carpenter tool shown in the figure?
A) Claw Hammer
B) Ball peen Hammer
C) Cross peenHammer
D) Straight peen Hammer
Q 100) Which of the following is not a type of furniture table?
A) Tea table
B) Computer table
C) Dining table
D) Excel table

Q 101) The power plane is essentially a ______________that drives a cutter bar.

A) high-speed motor

B) high-speed engine

C) Low-speed motor

D) None of these

Q 102) Sanding discs are installed using ______________.

A) Two wrenches of different sizes

B) Pressure-sensitive adhesive

C) Tension knob

D) Chuck key

Q 103) Identify the type of sanding machine shown in the figure.

A) Disc sander

B) Belt sander

C) Spindle sander

D) Gear sander

Q 104) In frame and panel construction, the outside vertical frame members is______.

A) Stiles

B) Rails

C) Lock rails

D) Mullion

Q 105) __________ windows are similar to the sliding doors and the shutter moves on the roller bearings, either

horizontally or vertically.

A) Sliding

B) Swinging

C) Rolling

D) Metal

Q 106) Sliding window is a type of window in which shutter moves____________.

A) Horizontally

B) Vertically

C) Either Horizontally or Vertically

D) None of these

Q 107) What is the main purpose of putty on a surface?

A) To fill any hairline cracks or holes on the surface of the wall

B) To create a uniform, levelled out surface ready for painting,

C) To prevent or reduce water seepage

D) All of these

Q 108) Name the accessory which is NOT used in drilling machine.

A) Tool holder

B) Sleeve

C) Socket

D) Drill chuck

Q 109) A _______________ is a power tool that can perform heavy-duty tasks such as drilling and chiseling hard

materials.

A) Rotary hammer

B) Jack plane

C) Belt sander

D) Reciprocating saw

Q 110) A wooden piece provided at the Ridge line of a sloping roof is known as the ______________.

A) Rafter

B) Ridge

C) Gable

D) Pitch

Q 111) In ___________ roofs, the common Rafter are provided to itself without any intermediate support.

A) Single

B) Double

C) Purlin

D) Trussed

Q 112) Figure given below shows a____________.

A) Queen post truss

B) King post truss

C) Both queen post and king post truss

D) None of these

Q 113) _______________ floors consists of single joist which are placed below the floor boards.

A) Single joint timber floor

B) Single joist timber floor

C) Single timber floor

D) Joist Floor

Q 114) The_____________size determines the coarseness of a sheet of sand paper.

A) Grit

B) Sand

C) Paper

D) Aluminium oxide

Q 115) Which tool is used by a carpenter for smoothing wood?

A) Plane

B) Chisel

C) Rip saw

D) Rasp

Q 116) Changes in wood moisture content can result in _____________of wood which can stress and crack coatings.

A) Swelling

B) Shrinkage

C) Swelling and shrinkage both

D) None of these

Q 117) ______________ is particularly effective at removing iron stains from wood.

A) Oxalic acid

B) Bleach

C) Water

D) Oil

Q 118) Primers are used___________.

A) Before painting

B) After painting

C) Together with paint

D) None of these

Q 119) The most durable varnish is_____________.

A) Oil varnish

B) Water varnish

C) Sprit varnish

D) All of these

Q 120) In Wood working CNC Router, CNC stands for _________________

A) Computer Numeric Control

B) Control Numeric Control

C) Computer Number Control

D) Counter Numeric Control

Q 121) In CNC operation G00 is a code for_______________.

A) Rapid positioning

B) Linear interpolation

C) Circular interpolation

D) None of these

Q 122) In CNC operation M00 is a code for_______________.

A) Program stop

B) Spindle start

C) Tool change

D) Coolant on

Q 123) What should be the moisture content when the density of timber is determined?

A) 12%

B) 18%

C) 20%

D) 22%

Q 124) The main component of wood turning lathe machine is___________.

A) Head stock and spindle

B) Tail stock and poppet barrel

C) Bed and tool rest

D) All of these

Q 125) Spindle turning involves turning stock held between the live center and the ____________.

A) Spur

B) tool rest

C) Headstock

D) Dead center

Q 126) The FIRST priority when working at a machine is-

A) Don t make any mistakes

B) Watch the other people around

C) Always thinking about safety

D) None of these

Q 127) Wax polish on wood comes under in which of the following category?

A) Evaporative

B) Clear

C) Water based

D) None of these

Answer Key

Level 1 Answer key

Question No.	Option	Question No.	Option	Question No.	Option	Question No.	Option	Question No.	Option
1	B	31	B	61	B	91	A	121	A
2	B	32	A	62	A	92	D	122	A
3	A	33	D	63	A	93	B	123	A
4	A	34	C	64	A	94	C	124	D
5	B	35	B	65	A	95	A	125	D
6	D	36	A	66	A	96	A	126	A
7	C	37	A	67	A	97	A	127	A
8	C	38	A	68	A	98	A		
9	C	39	D	69	A	99	A		
10	A	40	A	70	A	100	D		
11	B	41	D	71	A	101	A		
12	B	42	C	72	A	102	C		
13	C	43	B	73	D	103	A		
14	D	44	C	74	A	104	A		
15	C	45	A	75	D	105	A		
16	B	46	C	76	A	106	A		

17	A	47	B	77	A	107	D
18	C	48	C	78	A	108	A
19	C	49	D	79	A	109	A
20	C	50	A	80	A	110	B
21	B	51	C	81	A	111	A
22	A	52	B	82	A	112	A
23	B	53	B	83	A	113	B
24	B	54	A	84	A	114	A
25	A	55	A	85	A	115	A
26	A	56	A	86	A	116	C
27	A	57	C	87	A	117	A
28	C	58	A	88	A	118	A
29	A	59	D	89	D	119	A
30	D	60	A	90	D	120	A

Carpenter Level 2

Q 1) Softwood comes from evergreen trees that are called ....

A) Deciduous

B) Pine

C) Conifer

D) Fir

Q 2) What is the type of saw shown in figure given below?

A) Bow saw

B) Coping saw

C) Fretsaw

D) Compass saw

Q 3) The term kerf is asociated with..............

A) Files

B) Hammers

C) Saws

D) Chisels

Q 4) In the figure of a chisel shown below, what are A and B called as?

A) Edge and ferrule

B) Chisel blade and tang (inside handle)

C) Face and toe

D) Edge and toe

Q 5) Identify profiles A and B of the saws shown in figure given below.
और B को पहचानें । A

A) (A) Rip profile (B) Rip profile

B) (A) Cross-cut profile (B) Rip profile

C) (A) Rip profile (B) Cross-cut profile

D) (A) Cross-cut profile (B) Cross-cut profile

Q 6) Identify the type of shakes in the timber shown in figure given below.

A) Cup shakes

B) Heart shakes

C) Ring shakes

D) Star shakes

Q 7) Which one among these timbers has the highest density?

A) Teak

B) Deodar

C) Chir

D) Kail

Q 8) In natural seasoning of timber, it is difficult to reduce moisture content below ..

A) 15% / 15 %

B) 25% / 25 %

C) 35% / 35 %

D) 45% / 45%

Q 9) Application of creosote oil is one of the methods of preservation of timber. What is creosote?

A) it is a kind of paint

B) It is obtained by distillation of coal tar / यह तारकोल के आसवन से

C) It is a type of chemical salt like copper sulphate

D) It is like a lubricating oil

Q 10) In the figure given below, which one is corner half lap wood joint?

A) Joint 1

B) Joint 2

C) Joint 3

D) Joint 4

Q 11) Why is plastic resin glue NOT recommended for use on outdoor furniture?

A) It is not waterproof

B) It is not water resistant

C) It melts in sun

D) None of these

Q 12) What is the other name of pith in cross section of tree?

A) Xylastrus

B) Medulla

C) Parenchyma

D) Cycadophyta

Q 13) What is NOT recommended for exterior?

A) Marine board

B) Hardiflex

C) Ordinary plywood

D) Ficem

Q 14) What term is used to describe a wooden member built up of several layers of wood whose grain directions

are all substantially parallel?

A) Laminated timber

B) Treated lumber

C) Glued lumber

D) Chip board

Q 15) Manufactured boards are considered substitute for solid wood. What is NOT true about manufactured

boards?

A) They are stable

B) They are available in large sizes with uniform thickness

C) They are economical

D) They destroy tropical forests

Q 16) In fixing 12 mm plasterboards to a timber stud the most suitable fixing to use is

A) 50 mm oval

B) 35 mm stainless steel screws

C) 35 mm drywall screws

D) 75 mm roundheads

Q 17) The nail size unit is called ....

A) Numer

B) Penny Number

C) Weight in grams

D) None of these

Q 18) Long narrow hinges that run the full length of the two surfaces to which their leaves are joined, are called ....

A) Parliament hinges

B) Olive knuckle hinges

C) Invisible hinges

D) Piano hinges

Q 19) What is shown below is a piece of metal(Lock) for protection around a keyhole. It is called....

A) Cover

B) Face

C) Block

D) Escutcheon

Q 20) Identify the tool shown below which is being used to draw a large circle.

A) Scriber

B) Divider

C) Trammel

D) Caliper

Q 21) Pine wood is an example of ....

A) Deciduous

B) Conifer

C) White

D) Construction

Q 22) What is the type of joint shown in figure given below?

A) Rabbet joint

B) Mitre joint

C) Finger joint

D) Tongue ang groove joint

Q 23) What is the type of screw head shown in figure given below?

A) Philips

B) Tamper resistant

C) Torex

D) Allen

Q 24) What are the edges A and B (figure given below) of wooden pieces called?

A) (A) Bevelled (B) Tapered

B) (A) Bevelled (B) Chamfered

C) (A) Chamfered (B) Bevelled

D) (A) Chamfered (B) Tapered

Q 25) Figure below shows three planes. Name them correctly from left to right.

A) Jack plane; Smoothing plane; Try plane

B) Try plane; Smoothing plane; Jack plane

C) Smoothing plane; Jack plane; Try plane

D) Jack plane; Try plane; Smoothing plane

Q 26) Which statement is NOT true with regard to electrical seasoning of timber?

A) It is rapid method of seasoning

B) It uses low frequency electrical current

C) Its initial cost and maintenance cost is high

D) Timber, when green, offers less resistance to flow of electric current

Q 27) The conversion of timber as shown in figure given below is ....

A) Radial sawing

B) Quarter sawing

C) Tangential sawing

D) Baulking

Q 28) Where the door is required to swing both ways, the hinges used are ....

A) Double action hinges

B) Tee hinges

C) Friction hinges

D) Concealed hinges

Q 29) Figure given below shows a ....

A) Spring latch

B) Deadlocking latchbolt

C) Auxiliary latchbolt

D) Deadbolt

Q 30) The outer member of a truss that defines the envelope or shape is / are ....

A) Web

B) Chords

C) I - beam

D) Concrete

Q 31) In the figure of a truss shown in figure given below, strut is represented by ....

A) 1

B) 2

C) 3

D) 4

Q 32) In the figure of a table shown below, what is the part indicated by arrows?

A) Apron

B) Decorative bead

C) Cross member

D) Corner brace

Q 33) In the figure of stair shown below, what is A called?

A) Tread

B) Rise

C) Nosing

D) Teething

Q 34) In the figure of a stair shown below, what is the distance A called?

A) Staircase Step

B) Staircase Rise

C) Staircase Going

D) Staircase Space

Q 35) Figure below shows a mechanical tool which is called ....

A) Cat

B) Dog

C) Wolf

D) Sheep

Q 36) If a dispay board is to be hung on a wall, what will you use for hanging?

A) Screw eye

B) Square hook

C) Bench hook

D) Pincer

Q 37) Name the chisel-like tool with a curved or V-shaped blade used in wood crving.

A) Gauge

B) Gouge

C) Gamut

D) Gout

Q 38) What is the abrasive grit most often used on sandpaper?

A) Talc

B) Boron

C) Flint

D) Pumice

Q 39) What is the type of window shown in figure given below?

A) Sliding window

B) Louvered window

C) Casement window

D) Sash window

Q 40) Name the reciprocating electrical saw which is particularly useful in cutting curves.

A) Table saw

B) Scroll saw

C) Jigsaw

D) Band saw

Q 41) When using a plane or a chisel, wear ....

A) Gloves

B) Eye protection

C) Ear protection

D) Leg coverings

Q 42) Why is it important to turn the wooden piece on lathe manually before switching the power on?

A) To check for splinters and cracks

B) To check the tool rest clearance

C) To check that stock is not loose

D) All of the above

Q 43) Traversing the tool on a lathe parallel to the axis of the job is termed as ....

A) Cross feed

B) Longitudinal feed

C) Traverse feed

D) Depth feed

Q 44) What tool makes cuts at an angle to wood using a circular blade?

A) Chain saw

B) Mitre saw

C) Drill saw

D) Wonder saw

Q 45) What does a timber scribe (shown in figure below) do?

A) Hook onto nuts and bolts for easier removal

B) Used for marking trees and timber

C) Peel off dry wall

D) Used to cut wood into half

Q 46) The tool shown in figure given below is called ....

A) Sliding knife

B) Utility knife

C) Handy knife

D) Pincer knife

Q 47) The process by which a CNC machine is brought up to full operation is called ..

A) Dry run / ड? ई रन

B) Jogging / जॉगिंग

C) Zeroing / जीरोइंग

D) Initializing / इनिशलाइज़िंग

Q 48) Identify the tool shown in the figure.\चि? म? दशा?य े गय े औजार की पहचान कर?|

A) File

B) Chisel

C) Micrometer

D) Scriber

Q 49) Identify the tool shown in the figure.

A) Trying plane

B) Jack plane

C) Smoothing plane

D) Rebate plane

Q 50) Which of the following is the mechanical property of wood?

A) Strength

B) Toughness

C) Hardness

D) All of these

Q 51) What is Seasoning?

A) Process of water removing

B) Process of burning timber

C) Process of adding preservatives

D) Process of adding glaze

Q 52) Identify the type of joint shown in the figure.

A) Mitre joint

B) Finger join

C) Fish joint

D) Half lap joint

Q 53) Identify the type of joint shown in the figure.

A) Bridle joint

B) Finger joint

C) Fish joint

D) Half lap joint

Q 54) _________________ joints are employed to extend the width of board or

planks, which are placed edge to edge.

A) Widening

B) Angle

C) Lapped

D) Lengthening

Q 55) Which one of the following is a striking tool?

A) Hammer

B) Reamer

C) Jumper

D) Hammer bit

Q 56) The_________hole is drilled to receive the threaded portion of a wood screw.

A) Shank

B) Counter bore

C) Anchor

D) Conter sink

Q 57) Which board is made up of country wood strips of various sizes ranging from 18-38 mm in thickness?

A) Hard board

B) Ply board

C) Chip board

D) Block board

Q 58) What is the standard size of laminates?

A) 4 × 8

B) 3 × 7

C) 5 × 12

D) None of these

Q 59) The purpose of seasoning is not to reduce__________.

A) Hardness

B) Shrinkage

C) Weight

D) None of these

Q 60) Identify the hand tool shown in the figure?

A) Hand drill

B) Gimlet

C) Ratchet brace

D) Electric drill

Q 61) Which preservative is used for preservation of timber?\लकड़ी के संर?ण के लिए कौन सा संर?क उपयोग किया

जाता है?

A) Tar\टार

B) Paint\प?ट

C) Chemical salt\रसायनिक सा?

D) All of these\ये सभी

Q 62) In which direction, the feed roll moves the stock for planning in thickness planer?

A) Backward

B) Up direction

C) Forward

D) Down direction

Q 63) Identify the machine shown in the figure.

A) Chain mortiser

B) Portable electric jig saw

C) Disc sander

D) None of these

Q 64) Identify the hinge shown in the figure.

A) Butt hinge

B) Flush hinge

C) Lift off hinge

D) Tee hinge

Q 65) For filing cabinets which of the following lock is most suitable?

A) Cam lock

B) Pad lock

C) Mortise lock

D) Bored lock

Q 66) Identify the lock shown in the figure.

A) Mortise lock

B) Cylindrical lock

C) Bored lock

D) Unit lock

Q 67) Which among the following is the most rigid door frame?

A) Tenon and mortise

B) Canto mesa

C) Over lapping frame rabbeted

D) Dovetail

Q 68) The traditional ________ door shutters have inevitable problems of wrapping, rotting, painting and

maintenance.

A) Metal

B) Wooden

C) Glass

D) Plywood

Q 69) Which tool can produce face side and face edge in wood?

A) Jack plane

B) Belt sander

C) Reciprocating saw

D) Router

Q 70) Which one of the portable machine tool is very competent for cutting wood, composition board, veneer,

plastics, card board and leather?

A) Portable electric jig saw

B) Portable electric circular hand saw

C) Portable Sander

D) Portable electric Router

Q 71) What is king post truss?

A) A king post truss has two principal rafters, a tie beam,and a central vertical king post

B) A king post truss has one principal rafters,a tie beam,and a central vertical king post

C) A king post truss has two principal rafters and two central vertical king post

D) None of these

Q 72) Which of the following is not true for finish turning?

A) The tool used is a skew

B) Either cutting or scraping methods may be used

C) Work is begun at the center of the workpiece

D) None of these

Q 73) What the name of the chisel used for cutting rough surface quickly for turning on wood turning lathe?

A) Firmer chisel

B) Gauge chisel

C) Skew chisel

D) mortise chisel

Level 2 Answer key

Question No.	Option	Question No.	Option	Question No.	Option
1	C	31	D	61	D
2	D	32	A	62	C
3	C	33	C	63	A
4	B	34	C	64	A
5	C	35	B	65	A
6	D	36	B	66	A
7	A	37	B	67	A
8	A	38	C	68	B
9	B	39	D	69	A
10	A	40	C	70	A
11	A	41	B	71	A

12	B		42	D		72	D
13	C		43	B		73	B
14	A		44	B			
15	D		45	B			
16	C		46	B			
17	B		47	D			
18	D		48	D			
19	D		49	A			
20	C		50	D			
21	B		51	A			
22	A		52	D			
23	C		53	A			
24	C		54	A			
25	C		55	A			
26	B		56	C			
27	B		57	D			
28	A		58	A			
29	B		59	A			
30	B		60	C